Perfect Wedding Workbook

A Practical Guide for Brides

plan your budget

shop for your reception

gather your guest list

SUSAN SOUTHERLAND

ISBN: 0615834450
ISBN-13: 978-0615834450

Perfect Wedding Workbook

A Practical Guide for Brides

Introduction 2

Part 1: Pre-Planning 5
- Choosing Your Wedding Date 6
- Creating Your Guest List 6
- Creating Your Budget 14
- Hiring a Wedding Planner 21
- Choosing Your Wedding Type 25
- Choosing Your Wedding Colors 27
- Choosing Your Wedding Party 28
- Wedding Planning Timeline 32

Part 2: Shopping 37
- Interviewing Wedding Vendors 39
- Choosing Your Ceremony Site 40
- Choosing Your Reception Site 46
- Choosing Your Photographer and Videographer 52
- Choosing Your Florist 64
- Choosing Musicians 67
- Purchasing Your Wedding Attire 73
- Finding the Special Touches 74
- Negotiating Contracts 74

Part 3: Organizing 77
- Wedding Week Agenda 80
- Important Photo List 84
- Seating List 84
- Announcement List 86
- Inventory List 87

My Wedding Profile 89

My Notes 94

Index 101

Acknowledgements

I wish I could single out everyone who was involved in helping me write this book. In truth, I'd have to thank the thousands of couples who I've been lucky enough to help plan their weddings over the years. My experiences planning with them are what shaped my ideas and helped me write this book.

I also have to thank my team at *Just Marry!*; Karen Gingerich, Erin Calabritto, Faye Novick, Jennifer Haskell, and Diana Stylianou. You made it possible for me to write, and you gave me such great ideas and support. I hope I convey to each of you how lucky I am to work with you every day.

A big thank you to *Perfect Wedding Guide* for helping make my voice heard to a far greater audience than I could have ever done by myself. Tammy Elliott, in particular, you took a chance on me, believed in me, and helped me grow so much.

My final thank you is to my family. My father, Walter, and mother, Irma, who allowed me to try everything and always had faith that I could achieve great things. My brothers Allan (who I greatly miss) and Ron, and my sisters-in-law Beth and Nelly, thank you for being the village to my kids. I wouldn't have time to work, let alone write, if it weren't for you. Thank you to my husband, Scott, for being the best partner in life and in business that a woman could hope to have. And finally, thank you to my beautiful children, Larisa, Warren, Daniel, and Macy. In you I see that all things are possible, so I work extra hard to achieve my dreams. You are my inspiration and my anchors. I love you so much.

CONGRATULATIONS ON YOUR ENGAGEMENT! The coming months will be filled with exciting moments, beautiful memories, and *big* decisions. Sometimes these decisions will be very overwhelming. But don't panic! With easy-to-use resources from *Perfect Wedding Workbook* and *PerfectWeddingGuide.com,* planning your wedding will be both easy and perfectly delightful!

I find there are three components to planning a wedding; the business, the art, and the organization. This workbook deals primarily with the business and the organization (the not-so-glamorous stuff). I break down the business and organization into three sections for you: Pre-planning, Shopping, and Organizing.

Pre-planning will deal with items you'll need to address before you even spend a penny. This section includes:

- Choosing your wedding date
- Creating your guest list
- Creating your budget
- Hiring a wedding planner
- Choosing your wedding type
- Choosing your wedding colors
- Choosing your wedding party
- Wedding planning timeline

Once you have these tasks completed, you will move on to Shopping (so much fun!). This includes:

- Interviewing wedding vendors
- Choosing your ceremony site
- Choosing your reception site
- Choosing your photographer and videographer
- Choosing your florist
- Choosing musicians
- Purchasing your wedding attire
- Finding the special touches
- Negotiating contracts

Finally, you will need to Organize all the decisions you made. This section will help you create the following:

- Wedding week agenda
- Important photo list
- Seating list
- Announcement list
- Inventory list

On *PerfectWeddingGuide.com*, you can find my blog containing informative daily posts related to the top wedding planning issues. You may post questions there, or email me at susan.southerland@pwg.com. In addition to the useful tips found in my blog, you will also find valuable wedding planning tools, such as the *Budget Calculator*, *Guest List Manager*, *Timeline Creator*, and *Checklist Manager*. And I can't let you forget about the most useful tools used by my brides everywhere – my *Just Marry! Wedding Planning Color Wheel* and *Susan Southerland's Just Marry! Wedding Planning Secrets* on DVD! Both highly sought-after tools are available for purchase at *PerfectWeddingGuide.com*. Most importantly, always turn to *Perfect Wedding Guide's* directory for the best wedding planning vendors in your city!

With a little patience, a little sense of humor, and the many tools from *Perfect Wedding Guide*, you can rest assured that your wedding will be perfectly planned!

Best Wishes,
Susan Southerland
Wedding Expert for *Perfect Wedding Guide*

Part 1: Pre-Planning

Choosing Your Wedding Date

Choosing your wedding date is more important than you may think. The date you select will have the following impact on your wedding:

- *The time of day in which your ceremony starts.* For example, if you want a sunset or sunrise wedding, the time will vary throughout the year.
- *Your wedding location.* A garden ceremony on a cold January night in New York could be as miserable as a beachside ceremony on a hot August day in Florida! You must consider your guests' comfort when planning a wedding. If you've always dreamed of getting married outdoors, choose the date wisely.
- *The guests who may or may not attend.* Do you have friends and family with school-age children? Is your wedding party still in college? Remember, they might not be willing or able to travel during the school year.
- *Your wedding budget.* Certain times of the year are high-season for weddings. Vendors will charge a premium during these times. If you want to be cost-conscious, you should research which months have fewer weddings where yours will take place.
- *Availability of certain flowers and foods.* If you are an environmentally-conscious bride, or if you want to be cautious with your spending, you may want to check to see when your favorite items are in season where your wedding will take place.
- *The colors you choose.* I take a non-traditional stand on this. If your favorite color is bubble gum pink and you want your bridesmaids to wear it in January, I say go for it! But, if you are strictly traditional, you will want to decide whether your color scheme matches the season when you will wed.

Creating Your Guest List

I take a pretty no-nonsense approach when planning my couples' weddings. Before we go running around shopping for vendors, we have to build a foundation from which to start. That foundation is based on what we can spend and how that money is going to be spent.

The first step in determining your budget is to decide how many people you are going to invite and how many you expect to attend. I've created a guest list sheet for you to handwrite names, addresses, and phone numbers. Make copies of the list to cover the number of guests you plan to invite, or you can complete this guest list online at *My.PerfectWeddingGuide.com/Tools/GuestList/*

My Guest List

Name ________________________ Phone ________________________

Address ________________________ Gift received ________________________

☐ Attending ☐ Not attending ☐ Likely attending (1-most likely, 2-maybe, 3-probably not)

☐ Rehearsal dinner ☐ Brunch ☐ Needs transportation ☐ Special meal ☐ Thank you sent

Name ________________________ Phone ________________________

Address ________________________ Gift received ________________________

☐ Attending ☐ Not attending ☐ Likely attending (1-most likely, 2-maybe, 3-probably not)

☐ Rehearsal dinner ☐ Brunch ☐ Needs transportation ☐ Special meal ☐ Thank you sent

Name ________________________ Phone ________________________

Address ________________________ Gift received ________________________

☐ Attending ☐ Not attending ☐ Likely attending (1-most likely, 2-maybe, 3-probably not)

☐ Rehearsal dinner ☐ Brunch ☐ Needs transportation ☐ Special meal ☐ Thank you sent

Name ________________________ Phone ________________________

Address ________________________ Gift received ________________________

☐ Attending ☐ Not attending ☐ Likely attending (1-most likely, 2-maybe, 3-probably not)

☐ Rehearsal dinner ☐ Brunch ☐ Needs transportation ☐ Special meal ☐ Thank you sent

Name ________________________ Phone ________________________

Address ________________________ Gift received ________________________

☐ Attending ☐ Not attending ☐ Likely attending (1-most likely, 2-maybe, 3-probably not)

☐ Rehearsal dinner ☐ Brunch ☐ Needs transportation ☐ Special meal ☐ Thank you sent

My Guest List

Name ______________________ Phone ______________________

Address ______________________ Gift received ______________________

☐ Attending ☐ Not attending ☐ Likely attending (1-most likely, 2-maybe, 3-probably not)

☐ Rehearsal dinner ☐ Brunch ☐ Needs transportation ☐ Special meal ☐ Thank you sent

---

Name ______________________ Phone ______________________

Address ______________________ Gift received ______________________

☐ Attending ☐ Not attending ☐ Likely attending (1-most likely, 2-maybe, 3-probably not)

☐ Rehearsal dinner ☐ Brunch ☐ Needs transportation ☐ Special meal ☐ Thank you sent

---

Name ______________________ Phone ______________________

Address ______________________ Gift received ______________________

☐ Attending ☐ Not attending ☐ Likely attending (1-most likely, 2-maybe, 3-probably not)

☐ Rehearsal dinner ☐ Brunch ☐ Needs transportation ☐ Special meal ☐ Thank you sent

---

Name ______________________ Phone ______________________

Address ______________________ Gift received ______________________

☐ Attending ☐ Not attending ☐ Likely attending (1-most likely, 2-maybe, 3-probably not)

☐ Rehearsal dinner ☐ Brunch ☐ Needs transportation ☐ Special meal ☐ Thank you sent

---

Name ______________________ Phone ______________________

Address ______________________ Gift received ______________________

☐ Attending ☐ Not attending ☐ Likely attending (1-most likely, 2-maybe, 3-probably not)

☐ Rehearsal dinner ☐ Brunch ☐ Needs transportation ☐ Special meal ☐ Thank you sent

My Guest List

Name ______________________ Phone ______________________

Address ______________________ Gift received ______________________

☐ Attending ☐ Not attending ☐ Likely attending (1-most likely, 2-maybe, 3-probably not)

☐ Rehearsal dinner ☐ Brunch ☐ Needs transportation ☐ Special meal ☐ Thank you sent

Name ______________________ Phone ______________________

Address ______________________ Gift received ______________________

☐ Attending ☐ Not attending ☐ Likely attending (1-most likely, 2-maybe, 3-probably not)

☐ Rehearsal dinner ☐ Brunch ☐ Needs transportation ☐ Special meal ☐ Thank you sent

Name ______________________ Phone ______________________

Address ______________________ Gift received ______________________

☐ Attending ☐ Not attending ☐ Likely attending (1-most likely, 2-maybe, 3-probably not)

☐ Rehearsal dinner ☐ Brunch ☐ Needs transportation ☐ Special meal ☐ Thank you sent

Name ______________________ Phone ______________________

Address ______________________ Gift received ______________________

☐ Attending ☐ Not attending ☐ Likely attending (1-most likely, 2-maybe, 3-probably not)

☐ Rehearsal dinner ☐ Brunch ☐ Needs transportation ☐ Special meal ☐ Thank you sent

Name ______________________ Phone ______________________

Address ______________________ Gift received ______________________

☐ Attending ☐ Not attending ☐ Likely attending (1-most likely, 2-maybe, 3-probably not)

☐ Rehearsal dinner ☐ Brunch ☐ Needs transportation ☐ Special meal ☐ Thank you sent

My Guest List

Name ______________________ Phone ______________________

Address ______________________ Gift received ______________________

☐ Attending ☐ Not attending ☐ Likely attending (1-most likely, 2-maybe, 3-probably not)

☐ Rehearsal dinner ☐ Brunch ☐ Needs transportation ☐ Special meal ☐ Thank you sent

---

Name ______________________ Phone ______________________

Address ______________________ Gift received ______________________

☐ Attending ☐ Not attending ☐ Likely attending (1-most likely, 2-maybe, 3-probably not)

☐ Rehearsal dinner ☐ Brunch ☐ Needs transportation ☐ Special meal ☐ Thank you sent

---

Name ______________________ Phone ______________________

Address ______________________ Gift received ______________________

☐ Attending ☐ Not attending ☐ Likely attending (1-most likely, 2-maybe, 3-probably not)

☐ Rehearsal dinner ☐ Brunch ☐ Needs transportation ☐ Special meal ☐ Thank you sent

---

Name ______________________ Phone ______________________

Address ______________________ Gift received ______________________

☐ Attending ☐ Not attending ☐ Likely attending (1-most likely, 2-maybe, 3-probably not)

☐ Rehearsal dinner ☐ Brunch ☐ Needs transportation ☐ Special meal ☐ Thank you sent

---

Name ______________________ Phone ______________________

Address ______________________ Gift received ______________________

☐ Attending ☐ Not attending ☐ Likely attending (1-most likely, 2-maybe, 3-probably not)

☐ Rehearsal dinner ☐ Brunch ☐ Needs transportation ☐ Special meal ☐ Thank you sent

My Guest List

Name ______________________ Phone ______________________

Address ______________________ Gift received ______________________

☐ Attending ☐ Not attending ☐ Likely attending (1-most likely, 2-maybe, 3-probably not)

☐ Rehearsal dinner ☐ Brunch ☐ Needs transportation ☐ Special meal ☐ Thank you sent

Name ______________________ Phone ______________________

Address ______________________ Gift received ______________________

☐ Attending ☐ Not attending ☐ Likely attending (1-most likely, 2-maybe, 3-probably not)

☐ Rehearsal dinner ☐ Brunch ☐ Needs transportation ☐ Special meal ☐ Thank you sent

Name ______________________ Phone ______________________

Address ______________________ Gift received ______________________

☐ Attending ☐ Not attending ☐ Likely attending (1-most likely, 2-maybe, 3-probably not)

☐ Rehearsal dinner ☐ Brunch ☐ Needs transportation ☐ Special meal ☐ Thank you sent

Name ______________________ Phone ______________________

Address ______________________ Gift received ______________________

☐ Attending ☐ Not attending ☐ Likely attending (1-most likely, 2-maybe, 3-probably not)

☐ Rehearsal dinner ☐ Brunch ☐ Needs transportation ☐ Special meal ☐ Thank you sent

Name ______________________ Phone ______________________

Address ______________________ Gift received ______________________

☐ Attending ☐ Not attending ☐ Likely attending (1-most likely, 2-maybe, 3-probably not)

☐ Rehearsal dinner ☐ Brunch ☐ Needs transportation ☐ Special meal ☐ Thank you sent

My Guest List

Name ______________________ Phone ______________________

Address ______________________ Gift received ______________________

☐ Attending ☐ Not attending ☐ Likely attending (1-most likely, 2-maybe, 3-probably not)

☐ Rehearsal dinner ☐ Brunch ☐ Needs transportation ☐ Special meal ☐ Thank you sent

---

Name ______________________ Phone ______________________

Address ______________________ Gift received ______________________

☐ Attending ☐ Not attending ☐ Likely attending (1-most likely, 2-maybe, 3-probably not)

☐ Rehearsal dinner ☐ Brunch ☐ Needs transportation ☐ Special meal ☐ Thank you sent

---

Name ______________________ Phone ______________________

Address ______________________ Gift received ______________________

☐ Attending ☐ Not attending ☐ Likely attending (1-most likely, 2-maybe, 3-probably not)

☐ Rehearsal dinner ☐ Brunch ☐ Needs transportation ☐ Special meal ☐ Thank you sent

---

Name ______________________ Phone ______________________

Address ______________________ Gift received ______________________

☐ Attending ☐ Not attending ☐ Likely attending (1-most likely, 2-maybe, 3-probably not)

☐ Rehearsal dinner ☐ Brunch ☐ Needs transportation ☐ Special meal ☐ Thank you sent

---

Name ______________________ Phone ______________________

Address ______________________ Gift received ______________________

☐ Attending ☐ Not attending ☐ Likely attending (1-most likely, 2-maybe, 3-probably not)

☐ Rehearsal dinner ☐ Brunch ☐ Needs transportation ☐ Special meal ☐ Thank you sent

My Guest List

Name ______________________ Phone ______________________

Address ______________________ Gift received ______________________

☐ Attending ☐ Not attending ☐ Likely attending (1-most likely, 2-maybe, 3-probably not)

☐ Rehearsal dinner ☐ Brunch ☐ Needs transportation ☐ Special meal ☐ Thank you sent

Name ______________________ Phone ______________________

Address ______________________ Gift received ______________________

☐ Attending ☐ Not attending ☐ Likely attending (1-most likely, 2-maybe, 3-probably not)

☐ Rehearsal dinner ☐ Brunch ☐ Needs transportation ☐ Special meal ☐ Thank you sent

Name ______________________ Phone ______________________

Address ______________________ Gift received ______________________

☐ Attending ☐ Not attending ☐ Likely attending (1-most likely, 2-maybe, 3-probably not)

☐ Rehearsal dinner ☐ Brunch ☐ Needs transportation ☐ Special meal ☐ Thank you sent

Name ______________________ Phone ______________________

Address ______________________ Gift received ______________________

☐ Attending ☐ Not attending ☐ Likely attending (1-most likely, 2-maybe, 3-probably not)

☐ Rehearsal dinner ☐ Brunch ☐ Needs transportation ☐ Special meal ☐ Thank you sent

Name ______________________ Phone ______________________

Address ______________________ Gift received ______________________

☐ Attending ☐ Not attending ☐ Likely attending (1-most likely, 2-maybe, 3-probably not)

☐ Rehearsal dinner ☐ Brunch ☐ Needs transportation ☐ Special meal ☐ Thank you sent

Another low-tech way to organize your guest list is to put the information on the previous pages onto index cards and place them in a recipe card file. If you'd rather track on your computer, try creating a spreadsheet with the information provided. Or you can turn to the expert planning tools on *PerfectWeddingGuide.com* and allow the *Guest List Manager* to help you. The *Guest List Manager* will help organize far more than just who will be receiving your invitation. You will be able to track RSVP's, food choices and restrictions, and whether your guests will need sleeping accommodations and transportation. You will have access to the *Seating Chart Creator*, where you can hand over the messy maze of chairs and names to our manager. It's definitely a must!

Creating Your Budget

Now that we have estimated the number of guests who will be attending, we need some more information before creating your budget. During my many years of planning weddings, I have read over and over that certain percentages of the wedding budget should be reserved for particular services. I have found this theory doesn't always work. I have had clients who wanted a very expensive gown, so they spent less on flowers. I have had others whose most important service was photography, so they spent less on entertainment.

With that in mind, it's time to decide what items you want at your wedding, and which are most important to you. My team at *Just Marry!* created the questionnaire on the following pages. I encourage you to use the questionnaire to get a true sense of your priorities before creating your wedding budget.

Wedding Questionnaire **Identifying and ranking wedding components**

Rank the following items in order of importance, with number 1 being the most important item.
Within each category, circle the items you want included in your wedding and budget.

Rank	Item	To be paid by...
________	*Bridal Attire* *wedding gown • veil • alterations • pantyhose* *shoes • garter • crinoline • bra • purse • handkerchief*	____________
________	*Ceremony Decorations* *unity candle • pew arrangement • aisle runner* *altar arrangement • sand ceremony • chair decorations*	____________

Wedding Questionnaire **Identifying and ranking wedding components**

Rank	Item	To be paid by...
________	*Ceremony Venue* *officiant • musicians • custodian • counseling • site • soloist*	________________
________	*Entertainment* *reception • cocktail hour*	________________
________	*Floral Preservation* *bride's bouquet • parents' flowers*	________________
________	*Hair and Makeup* *trial run • bride • wedding party • mothers • others*	________________
________	*Honeymoon* *trip • excursions • parking • spending money*	________________
________	*Miscellaneous* *bride's ring • groom's ring • disposable cameras* *dance lessons • wedding website • Cake knife* *cake topper • Ketubah • ring bearer pillow* *marriage license • gift for bride • gift for groom* *bridal attendants' gifts • groom attendants' gifts* *bridesmaids' luncheon • toasting glasses •* *sparklers/bubbles • rehearsal dinner • favors*	________________
________	*Personal Flowers* *bride's bouquet • maid of honor bouquet* *bridesmaids' bouquets • throw bouquet* *flower girl bouquet • groom's boutonniere • best man's bout.* *groomsmen bouts. • fathers' bouts. • grandfathers' bouts.* *mothers' corsages • grandmothers' corsages* *sign-in book corsage • reader corsage*	________________
________	*Photography* *package • overtime • tax • parents' album • bridal portrait* *reprints • engagement photos • trash the dress session* *boudoir session • high-resolution copyright-free DVD*	________________

Wedding Questionnaire — Identifying and ranking wedding components

Rank	Item	To be paid by...
______	*Reception Decorations* *centerpieces • head table flowers • cake flowers* *trees • florals • linens • lighting • furniture rental* *chargers • specialty chairs*	______
______	*Reception Site* *hall tables • tents • china/crystal • dance floor • beverage* *cocktail hour food • cocktail hour bar • specialty cocktail* *appetizer • salad/soup • intermezzo • plated entrée* *food stations • buffet • late-night snack • candy bar* *dessert presentation • cookie bar • service people*	______
______	*Stationery* *invitations • announcements • printed envelopes • envelope liners* *informals • reception cards • response sets • at home cards* *map cards • colored ink • place cards • monogram die* *return address card • calligraphy • cocktail napkins* *luncheon napkins • dinner napkins • weekend programs* *ceremony programs • shipping/postage*	______
______	*Transportation* *bride and groom • wedding party • guests*	______
______	*Videography* *video package • video overtime • extra videos • tax*	______
______	*Wedding Cake* *total cake • tip • delivery/set up • sugar flowers*	______
______	*Wedding Planner* *full-service • day-of • ceremony assistance*	______

Now that you know your priorities, it's time to create your budget. Over the years, I have found that food and beverage for the reception typically accounts for half the total budget. For the sake of estimating, divide your budget in half and put that amount in the reception column. Next, assign amounts to all the other services you would like, based on your priorities. If you want a huge amount of flowers, make sure you assign a significant amount of your budget to the floral category. If having favors at your wedding isn't important to you, eliminate it from your budget so you have more money for the services you do want.

The following pages include a sample budget worksheet. You can use this to get an idea of what you plan to spend on all the items in your wedding. However, the budget is ever-changing. As you hire services and vendors, your dollar amounts will evolve. If you want to make your budget an effective tool, I suggest using the *Budget Calculator* at *My.PerfectWeddingGuide.com/Tools/BudgetCalculator/*. It will assign amounts to each service based on your overall budget, and it will allow you to make changes as you make new decisions.

Whether you prefer to use an online tool or do it by hand, you should revise your budget every time you hire a vendor or purchase an item, and remember to change the dollar values. Before going to your next appointment, check to ensure that you know how much money you have available for that vendor or service. Keeping to your budget is all about making adjustments as you spend and keeping an eye on your bottom line. If you spend more on one item, you will have to spend less on another. It's that simple!

Wedding Budget

BRIDAL ATTIRE	Budget	Actual
• Alterations	$______	$______
• Bra	$______	$______
• Crinoline	$______	$______
• Garter	$______	$______
• Handkerchief	$______	$______
• Pantyhose	$______	$______
• Purse	$______	$______
• Shoes	$______	$______
• Veil	$______	$______
• Wedding gown	$______	$______

CEREMONY DECORATIONS	Budget	Actual
• Aisle runner	$______	$______
• Altar arrangement	$______	$______
• Chair decorations	$______	$______
• Pew arrangement	$______	$______
• Sand ceremony	$______	$______
• Unity candle	$______	$______

CEREMONY VENUE	Budget	Actual
• Counseling	$______	$______
• Custodian	$______	$______
• Musicians	$______	$______
• Officiant	$______	$______
• Site	$______	$______
• Soloist	$______	$______

ENTERTAINMENT	Budget	Actual
• Cocktail hour	$______	$______
• Reception	$______	$______

FLORAL PRESERVATION	Budget	Actual
• Bride's bouquet	$______	$______
• Parents' flowers	$______	$______

HAIR AND MAKEUP	Budget	Actual
• Bride	$______	$______
• Mothers	$______	$______
• Others	$______	$______
• Trial run	$______	$______
• Wedding party	$______	$______

HONEYMOON	Budget	Actual
• Excursions	$______	$______
• Parking	$______	$______
• Spending money	$______	$______
• Trip	$______	$______

MISCELLANEOUS	Budget	Actual
• Bridal attendants' gifts	$______	$______
• Bride's ring	$______	$______
• Bridesmaids' luncheon	$______	$______
• Cake knife	$______	$______
• Cake topper	$______	$______
• Dance lessons	$______	$______
• Disposable cameras	$______	$______
• Favors	$______	$______
• Gift for bride	$______	$______
• Gift for groom	$______	$______
• Groom attendants' gifts	$______	$______
• Groom's ring	$______	$______
• Ketubah	$______	$______

Wedding Budget (continued)

MISCELLANEOUS (cont.)	Budget	Actual
• Marriage license	$_____	$_____
• Rehearsal dinner	$_____	$_____
• Ring bearer pillow	$_____	$_____
• Sparklers/bubbles	$_____	$_____
• Toasting glasses	$_____	$_____
• Wedding website	$_____	$_____

PERSONAL FLOWERS	Budget	Actual
• Best man's boutonniere	$_____	$_____
• Bride's bouquet	$_____	$_____
• Bridesmaids' bouquets	$_____	$_____
• Fathers' boutonnieres	$_____	$_____
• Flower girl bouquet	$_____	$_____
• Grandfathers' bouts.	$_____	$_____
• Grandmothers' corsages	$_____	$_____
• Groom's boutonniere	$_____	$_____
• Groomsmen boutonnieres	$_____	$_____
• Maid of honor bouquet	$_____	$_____
• Mothers' corsages	$_____	$_____
• Reader corsage	$_____	$_____
• Sign-in book corsage	$_____	$_____
• Throw bouquet	$_____	$_____

PHOTOGRAPHY	Budget	Actual
• Boudoir session	$_____	$_____
• Bridal portrait	$_____	$_____
• Engagement photos	$_____	$_____
• Hi-res copyright-free DVD	$_____	$_____
• Overtime	$_____	$_____
• Package	$_____	$_____
• Parents' album	$_____	$_____

PHOTOGRAPHY (cont.)	Budget	Actual
• Reprints	$_____	$_____
• Tax	$_____	$_____
• Trash the dress session	$_____	$_____

RECEPTION DECORATIONS	Budget	Actual
• Cake flowers	$_____	$_____
• Centerpieces	$_____	$_____
• Chargers	$_____	$_____
• Florals	$_____	$_____
• Furniture rental	$_____	$_____
• Head table flowers	$_____	$_____
• Lighting	$_____	$_____
• Linens	$_____	$_____
• Specialty chairs	$_____	$_____
• Trees	$_____	$_____

RECEPTION SITE	Budget	Actual
• Appetizer	$_____	$_____
• Beverage	$_____	$_____
• Buffet	$_____	$_____
• Candy bar	$_____	$_____
• China/crystal	$_____	$_____
• Cocktail hour bar	$_____	$_____
• Cocktail hour food	$_____	$_____
• Cookie bar	$_____	$_____
• Dance floor	$_____	$_____
• Dessert presentation	$_____	$_____
• Food stations	$_____	$_____
• Hall tables	$_____	$_____
• Intermezzo	$_____	$_____

Wedding Budget (continued)

RECEPTION SITE (cont.)	Budget	Actual
• Late-night snack	$______	$______
• Plated entrée	$______	$______
• Salad/soup	$______	$______
• Service people	$______	$______
• Specialty cocktail	$______	$______
• Tents	$______	$______

STATIONERY	Budget	Actual
• Announcements	$______	$______
• At home cards	$______	$______
• Calligraphy	$______	$______
• Ceremony programs	$______	$______
• Cocktail napkins	$______	$______
• Colored ink	$______	$______
• Dinner napkins	$______	$______
• Envelope liners	$______	$______
• Informals	$______	$______
• Invitations	$______	$______
• Luncheon napkins	$______	$______
• Map cards	$______	$______
• Monogram die	$______	$______
• Place cards	$______	$______
• Printed envelopes	$______	$______
• Reception cards	$______	$______
• Response sets	$______	$______
• Return address card	$______	$______
• Shipping/postage	$______	$______
• Weekend programs	$______	$______

TRANSPORTATION	Budget	Actual
• Bride and groom	$______	$______
• Guests	$______	$______
• Wedding party	$______	$______

VIDEOGRAPHY	Budget	Actual
• Extra videos	$______	$______
• Tax	$______	$______
• Video overtime	$______	$______
• Video package	$______	$______

WEDDING CAKE	Budget	Actual
• Delivery/set up	$______	$______
• Sugar flowers	$______	$______
• Tip	$______	$______
• Total cake	$______	$______

WEDDING PLANNER	Budget	Actual
• Ceremony assistance	$______	$______
• Day-of	$______	$______
• Full-service	$______	$______

Hiring a Wedding Planner (Coordinator, Consultant)

This is a very personal decision. As a long-time planner, I, of course, am a big fan of wedding planners. A great planner will help you with tasks that you don't particularly enjoy doing, and she will have good ideas on vendors who will work well with your budget and style. *Most importantly*, on your wedding day she will relieve you, and your family and friends, of the hours of hard work that goes into making your wedding day run smoothly. You will be able to relax and enjoy your wedding day knowing your wedding wishes and dreams will take place just as you planned. Your planner is a budget counselor, advocate, sounding board, advisor, mediator, and problem solver! On one of the most important days of one's life, every bride and groom will benefit extraordinarily from having a multi-talented planner.

Planners work in many different ways with their clients. Some will only work with you if you want her to plan your wedding from beginning to end. Others will work with you just on your wedding day. *PerfectWeddingGuide.com* is filled with lists of professional planners across the mass of budget and service ranges. You may want to interview a few to see if one would make your wedding day just a little better and stress-free.

If you decide to interview a planner, I highly recommend using the questions on the following pages. I suggest these questions because it's very important to have a conversation and be able to talk freely with your planner. Aside from the planner's experience and expertise, his or her personality is the key to a perfect wedding day. Even if you are completely happy and walking on air on your wedding day, there is no doubt the day will have some stress. You want to make sure the planner who will be at your side is someone who soothes you and makes you feel comfortable. If anything about the planner screams "control freak," or makes you just plain uneasy, walk away. There are many, many other planners available to interview.

Wedding Planner Comparison	Planner 1
Name of planner	
Address	
Phone	
Email	
Referred by	
How long have you been in business?	
Do you have any professional affiliations?	
Do you participate in continuing education?	
Your responsibilities during planning?	
Your responsibilities on my wedding day?	
Do you have a staff?	
Will I be working with you or a staff member?	
Fees	
Payment schedule	
How many assistants will attend my wedding?	
How do I rate this planner? (circle one)	No way Almost Perfect Perfect!

Wedding Planner Comparison	Planner 2
Name of planner	
Address	
Phone	
Email	
Referred by	
How long have you been in business?	
Do you have any professional affiliations?	
Do you participate in continuing education?	
Your responsibilities during planning?	
Your responsibilities on my wedding day?	
Do you have a staff?	
Will I be working with you or a staff member?	
Fees	
Payment schedule	
How many assistants will attend my wedding?	
How do I rate this planner? (circle one)	No way Almost Perfect Perfect!

Wedding Planner Comparison	Planner 3
Name of planner	
Address	
Phone	
Email	
Referred by	
How long have you been in business?	
Do you have any professional affiliations?	
Do you participate in continuing education?	
Your responsibilities during planning?	
Your responsibilities on my wedding day?	
Do you have a staff?	
Will I be working with you or a staff member?	
Fees	
Payment schedule	
How many assistants will attend my wedding?	
How do I rate this planner? (circle one)	No way Almost Perfect Perfect!

If you decide a wedding planner isn't for you, the tools in this workbook will be instrumental in preparing you for your wedding day. However, you *do not* want to be the one in charge of your wedding! Take all your information – your contracts, swatches, checklists, and notes – and give them to a friend, or someone responsible, two weeks prior to your wedding. Make sure he or she knows everything you want at your wedding. That person should become the contact for your vendors and catering manager. You need to have one person in charge, and that person shouldn't be you!

Choosing Your Wedding Type

When you envision your wedding, do you see fancy and formal, or simple and casual? Do you want your guests in tuxedos or khakis? Answering a few simple questions will help you determine the ideal time of day for your wedding, the location, and the types of services you will need. Take a peek at the questionnaire on the following page to see which type of wedding best fits your style.

What's Your Wedding Type?

When you imagine your wedding gown, what does it look like?

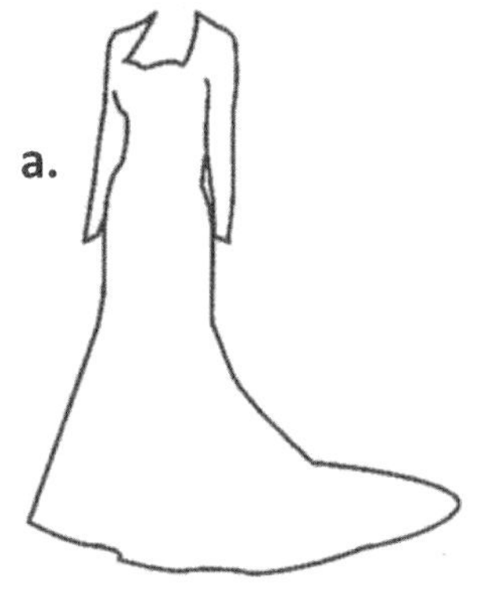

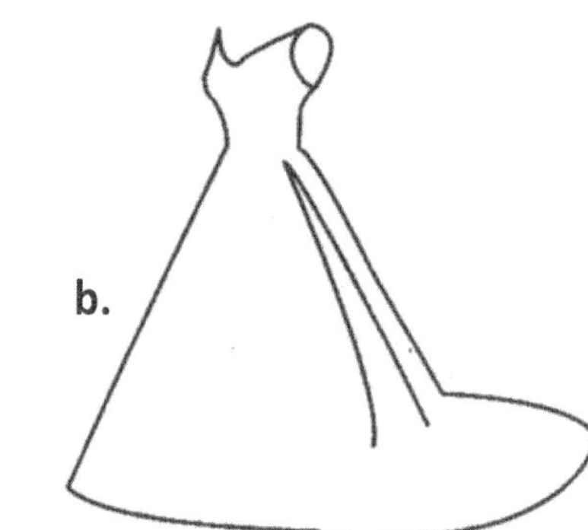

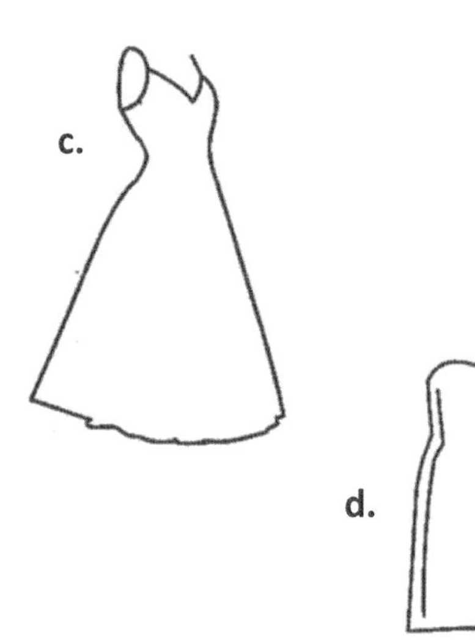

When you imagine your guests, what are they wearing?

a. Gowns and tuxedos

b. Cocktail dresses and suits

c. Casual dresses and jackets

d. Jeans or khakis

What time of day do you want to celebrate?

a. Dinner time

b. Mid-morning

c. Lunch time

d. Late night

Where do you envision your wedding ceremony?

a. Place of worship

b. Hotel ballroom

c. Museum or other landmark

d. Garden or beach

If you chose mostly "A" answers, you probably want a very formal wedding. A ceremony followed by a cocktail hour, dinner, and dancing, is just right for you.

If you chose mostly "B" answers, you may still want a formal wedding, but it doesn't have to be ultra-formal. You may like a brunch or cocktail hour followed by dinner and dancing.

If you chose mostly "C" answers, you have many options. You would be just as comfortable with a formal ceremony followed by a formal dinner, or a slightly more casual affair including a fabulous brunch or lunch reception.

If you chose mostly "D" answers, a formal affair would drive you crazy! Try a more whimsical event, like an early morning beach ceremony followed by breakfast, or a late-night dessert reception. Of course, you could still do a traditional dinner reception, but cut down on the formalities.

Now that you have an idea of the type of wedding that fits your personality, you should keep in mind that the more formal the affair, the more expensive it tends to be. Also, weddings today don't follow the old traditional mindset. If you have your heart set on something formal, but need to watch your pennies, do a late-night dessert reception. Guests will feel comfortable wearing formal attire, but you can scale back on the food and beverage you provide. This will save you thousands of dollars. Don't be afraid to think outside the box. Create the wedding that reflects *YOUR* personality and style!

Choosing Your Wedding Colors

This may be the easiest task of all. Look at your wardrobe and look to photos of weddings that appeal to you. Once you find a core color you like, use fabric swatches or paint chips to determine which colors complement your core color the most. I suggest using my *Just Marry! Wedding Planning Color Wheel*, which was designed so my brides can visualize and match their colors to swatches while on-the-go. There is a brief explanation on the back of the wheel discussing the different types of color schemes, and the wheel is compact and portable. You can easily take the color wheel with you when you're selecting bridesmaids' dresses, flowers, linens, and lighting.

Choosing Your Wedding Party

Before you start shopping, you must know the number of attendants you will be having. So now is the time to ask your friends and family to stand up with you at your wedding! My clients have shared some wonderful stories of how they invited their wedding parties to participate. Some sent formal invitations, others had dinner parties. Try to come up with something fun and creative to ask your friends to participate. Remember, everything you do will create a wonderful memory leading up to your big day! Once you have asked, and your wedding party has agreed, complete the form provided on the following pages. This form is a simple layout I always use with my brides and grooms.

Keep in mind that accepting an invitation to be in your wedding party usually requires a significant financial obligation. Typically, bridesmaids and groomsmen will have to purchase special attire for the wedding day, and travel to the wedding. They may also incur expenses for throwing parties, having their hair and makeup done (or a shave and haircut for the gentlemen). Don't be offended if one of your good friends has to turn you down for financial reasons. Also, be considerate when choosing your attire so it isn't overly expensive. If you have the financial means, you may want to consider reserving some of your wedding budget to help your wedding party with their expenses.

Wedding Party Contact Information

Maid of Honor

Name ________________________________

Phone ________________________________

Email ________________________________

Address ________________________________

Best Man

Name ________________________________

Phone ________________________________

Email ________________________________

Address ________________________________

Bridesmaid 1

Name ________________________________

Phone ________________________________

Email ________________________________

Address ________________________________

Groomsman 1

Name ________________________________

Phone ________________________________

Email ________________________________

Address ________________________________

Bridesmaid 2

Name ________________________________

Phone ________________________________

Email ________________________________

Address ________________________________

Groomsman 2

Name ________________________________

Phone ________________________________

Email ________________________________

Address ________________________________

Wedding Party Contact Information (continued)

Bridesmaid 3

Name ______________________

Phone______________________

Email ______________________

Address ____________________

Groomsman 3

Name ______________________

Phone______________________

Email ______________________

Address ____________________

Bridesmaid 4

Name ______________________

Phone______________________

Email ______________________

Address ____________________

Groomsman 4

Name ______________________

Phone______________________

Email ______________________

Address ____________________

Bridesmaid 5

Name ______________________

Phone______________________

Email ______________________

Address ____________________

Groomsman 5

Name ______________________

Phone______________________

Email ______________________

Address ____________________

Wedding Party Contact Information (continued)

Bridesmaid 6

Name ______________________

Phone______________________

Email ______________________

Address ____________________

Groomsman 6

Name ______________________

Phone______________________

Email ______________________

Address ____________________

Flower Girl

Name ______________________

Phone______________________

Email ______________________

Address ____________________

Ring Bearer

Name ______________________

Phone______________________

Email ______________________

Address ____________________

Usher 1

Name ______________________

Phone______________________

Email ______________________

Address ____________________

Guest Book Attendant 1

Name ______________________

Phone______________________

Email ______________________

Address ____________________

Wedding Planning Timeline

Congratulations! You have now made some of the most important decisions. These will be the foundation of the entire wedding planning process. It is almost time to move on and do some shopping! The final step in this section is to create a timeline to help you keep on track during the wedding planning process. Below is a copy of the timeline I use with my clients. If you desire something a little more interactive, check out the great tools on *PerfectWeddingGuide.com*. You'll find the *Timeline Manager*, which automatically places the dates in the timeline for you, based on your wedding date. It's a great tool for keeping you on track!

If you start planning less than six months prior to your big day, don't let this timeline scare you! You will just have to work a little faster. You can still use the timeline to stay organized; just check items off your list in the order given as quickly as you can get them done.

Wedding Planning Checklist

Est. Completion Date	Task	Actual date
	At least six months prior to wedding	
____________	Complete wedding party contact list and give to planner	____________
____________	Put crucial deadlines provided by planner into calendar	____________
____________	Approve spending allocation and give to planner	____________
____________	Determine type of wedding	____________
____________	Determine color scheme	____________
____________	Finish guest list including addresses and phone numbers	____________
____________	Purchase wedding gown	____________
____________	Purchase bridesmaids' dresses	____________
____________	Announce engagement in newspaper	____________
____________	Send save-the-date and reservation forms	____________

Wedding Planning Checklist (continued)

Est. Completion Date	Task	Actual date
	At least five months prior to wedding	
________	Determine ceremony site	________
________	Determine reception site	________
________	Reserve hotel rooms for out of town guests	________
________	Select photographer	________
________	Select videographer	________
________	Select ceremony musician	________
________	Select reception band/musician/DJ	________
________	Schedule engagement portrait	________
	At least four months prior to wedding	
________	Select florist	________
________	Select linen company	________
________	Select pastry chef	________
________	Select groom and groomsmen attire	________
________	Order invitations/stationery/announcements	________
________	Invitations	________
________	Return address envelopes	________
________	Liners	________
________	Map cards	________
________	Response cards	________
________	Thank you notes	________
________	Reception cards	________
________	Napkins	________
________	Programs	________
________	Place cards	________
________	Select calligrapher	________
________	Meet with caterer/catering manager and plan menu	________

Wedding Planning Checklist (continued)

Est. Completion Date	Task	Actual date
	At least three months prior to wedding	
____________	Plan honeymoon	____________
____________	Send invitations to calligrapher	____________
____________	Enroll at bridal registries and advise planner	____________
____________	Meet with florist and make final floral selections	____________
____________	Make final linen selections	____________
	At least two months prior to wedding	
____________	Confirm wedding rehearsal time	____________
____________	Attend menu tasting	____________
____________	Make a list of songs you do/do not want at reception	____________
____________	Select wedding favors	____________
____________	Mail invitations	____________
____________	Select hair and makeup artist and schedule trial run	____________
____________	Arrange wedding day transportation	____________
____________	Select wedding favors	____________
____________	Purchase bridal party accessories	____________
____________	Flower girl basket	____________
____________	Ring bearer pillow	____________
____________	Guest book and pen	____________
____________	Cake knife and server	____________
____________	Toasting flutes	____________
____________	Other	____________
____________	Plan rehearsal dinner	____________
____________	Select ceremony music	____________
____________	Discuss ceremony with officiant and choose readings	____________
____________	Apply for marriage license	____________

Wedding Planning Checklist (continued)

Est. Completion Date	Task	Actual date
	At least one month prior to wedding	
______________	Schedule final fitting	______________
______________	Contact floral and gown preservationists	______________
______________	Design transportation inserts for out of town guests	______________
	Less than one month prior to wedding	
______________	Give music sheets to ceremony musicians	______________
______________	Give music sheets to reception musicians	______________
______________	Give checklist for wedding photos to photographer	______________
______________	Approve vendor wedding day schedule	______________
______________	Approve wedding party schedule for wedding day	______________
______________	Break-in shoes	______________
______________	Follow up on guests who did not respond	______________
______________	Meet with planner to go over details	______________
______________	Pay balances due on services required before wedding	______________
______________	Give final head count to planner	______________
______________	Set seating arrangements	______________
______________	Write place cards	______________
______________	Write thank you notes for gifts as they come	______________
	Day before wedding	
______________	Attend rehearsal	______________
______________	Bring marriage license to rehearsal	______________
______________	Go to bed early	______________
	Wedding day!	
______________	Follow wedding day schedule	______________

Okay ladies, it's time to do what we do best… LET'S GO SHOPPING!

Part 2: Shopping

You've done a great deal of soul-searching during the pre-planning process. You know how much you have to spend, and how you want to spend it based on your priorities and budget. You know the formality and type of wedding you want to have, and you have decided on the colors you want to use. Now it's time to find the location where your wedding will take place, and the vendors who will service your wedding day.

Before you start the interviewing process, I highly suggest you do the following:

- Do preliminary research on *PerfectWeddingGuide.com*.
- Check vendor websites and try to narrow down your options to three possibilities.
- Check websites for potential wedding locations and try to narrow down your options to three possibilities.
- Do a phone interview before going on a site visit. This will save you time and gas.
- Visit the vendors and potential wedding locations to make sure everything looks as good in person as it does on the website.
- Make sure you are happy with the staff. You don't want an overbearing vendor or location coordinator making you a wreck on your wedding day.
- Of course, if not one of the first three is perfect, choose three more!
- Once you find a location or vendor that is perfect, record the information in *My Wedding Profile* located in the back of this book.

Interviewing Wedding Vendors

The following pages are dedicated to interviewing potential wedding vendors. Some brides find this process intimidating. But I assure you, wedding vendors love the interview process. It is our opportunity to show off our work, as well as show you how we can fit into your wedding day vision. Any good wedding vendor welcomes the interview process and isn't afraid to answer difficult questions.

Some of the questions in my checklist may seem a little odd. I included those questions to help spark a conversation. You don't have to stick to my questions exclusively. The ones regarding availability, price, qualifications, and contract information shouldn't change. However, questions about each vendor's favorite type of wedding or wedding style can be changed. Think about what it is you really want to know about your potential vendor and have a conversation. You will learn volumes about each vendor's personality and your comfort level with the vendor.

Go to each appointment prepared with your questions and mine, and bring this workbook to write down your answers. Make little notes about each vendor's personality, too, so that you can remember your thoughts later.

If interviewing really makes you nervous, take someone with you for moral support. Also, schedule your meetings so that your favorite vendor is last on your list. That way, you will have a little practice before seeing your favorite. I truly believe that once you get going, your nervousness will go away. So don't let this process cause you unnecessary stress. If you come up with great interview questions of your own, share them with me! Other brides will love to learn from you. You can email your questions to me directly at susan.southerland@pwg.com, or post on my Facebook page.

Choosing Your Ceremony Site

Your ceremony site is very important – after all, it will be immortalized in all your wedding photos. If you belong to a church or synagogue, your selection will be an easy one. You will still need to get answers to the questions below, so don't skip this important information gathering step. If your ceremony is going to take place at a location other than your regular place of worship, you can seek the location that fits your personality and style perfectly.

Ceremony Site Comparison	Site 1
Site name	
Address	
Phone	
Email	
Website	
Contact person	
Available for my wedding?	
What times are available?	
Rental fee	
Clergy fee	
Pre-marital counseling fee	
Ceremony coordinator fee	
Custodial fee	
Musician fee	
Other fees	
When are fees due?	
Are pre-marital classes required?	
Fee for pre-marital class	
Date and time for pre-marital class	

Ceremony Site Comparison (continued)	Site 1
[1]Restrictions and requirements	
Rehearsal availability time	
How many guests can the site accommodate?	
Ample parking?	
Room for bride and wedding party to dress?	
Room for groom and wedding party to dress?	
[2]How long can I use the site?	
If outdoors, is there a good indoor backup?	
Is site decorated differently on wedding day?	
[3]What services does the site provide?	
How do I rate this site? (circle one)	No way Almost Perfect Perfect!

[1] Make sure you get a list of requirements for your place of worship. Most places of worship will have a list of music, photography, videography, décor, and attire restrictions. These are very important to have *before* you begin shopping for vendors, gowns, and tuxedos.

[2] You need to find out when vendors can get into the site to set up, when you can get in to dress (or do you have to arrive ready to walk down the aisle), when guests need to leave, when your decorations need to be removed, and how long you can take post-wedding photos.

[3] Some sites provide audio equipment, seating, ceremony coordinator, officiant, candelabras, and other décor. Find out what your potential site has available. It may save you money.

Ceremony Site Comparison	Site 2
Site name	
Address	
Phone	
Email	
Website	
Contact person	
Available for my wedding?	
What times are available?	
Rental fee	
Clergy fee	
Pre-marital counseling fee	
Ceremony coordinator fee	
Custodial fee	
Musician fee	
Other fees	
When are fees due?	
Are pre-marital classes required?	
Fee for pre-marital class	
Date and time for pre-marital class	

Ceremony Site Comparison (continued)	Site 2
[1]Restrictions and requirements	
Rehearsal availability time	
How many guests can the site accommodate?	
Ample parking?	
Room for bride and wedding party to dress?	
Room for groom and wedding party to dress?	
[2]How long can I use the site?	
If outdoors, is there a good indoor backup?	
Is site decorated differently on wedding day?	
[3]What services does the site provide?	
How do I rate this site? (circle one)	No way Almost Perfect Perfect!

[1] Make sure you get a list of requirements for your place of worship. Most places of worship will have a list of music, photography, videography, décor, and attire restrictions. These are very important to have *before* you begin shopping for vendors, gowns, and tuxedos.

[2] You need to find out when vendors can get into the site to set up, when you can get in to dress (or do you have to arrive ready to walk down the aisle), when guests need to leave, when your decorations need to be removed, and how long you can take post-wedding photos.

[3] Some sites provide audio equipment, seating, ceremony coordinator, officiant, candelabras, and other décor. Find out what your potential site has available. It may save you money.

Ceremony Site Comparison	Site 3
Site name	
Address	
Phone	
Email	
Website	
Contact person	
Available for my wedding?	
What times are available?	
Rental fee	
Clergy fee	
Pre-marital counseling fee	
Ceremony coordinator fee	
Custodial fee	
Musician fee	
Other fees	
When are fees due?	
Are pre-marital classes required?	
Fee for pre-marital class	
Date and time for pre-marital class	

Ceremony Site Comparison (continued)	Site 3
[1]Restrictions and requirements	
Rehearsal availability time	
How many guests can the site accommodate?	
Ample parking?	
Room for bride and wedding party to dress?	
Room for groom and wedding party to dress?	
[2]How long can I use the site?	
If outdoors, is there a good indoor backup?	
Is site decorated differently on wedding day?	
[3]What services does the site provide?	
How do I rate this site? (circle one)	No way Almost Perfect Perfect!

[1] Make sure you get a list of requirements for your place of worship. Most places of worship will have a list of music, photography, videography, décor, and attire restrictions. These are very important to have *before* you begin shopping for vendors, gowns, and tuxedos.

[2] You need to find out when vendors can get into the site to set up, when you can get in to dress (or do you have to arrive ready to walk down the aisle), when guests need to leave, when your decorations need to be removed, and how long you can take post-wedding photos.

[3] Some sites provide audio equipment, seating, ceremony coordinator, officiant, candelabras, and other décor. Find out what your potential site has available. It may save you money.

Choosing Your Reception Site

Your reception site should reflect your personality and style. Make certain you love the way the location looks, and that the menu options suit your taste.

Reception Site Comparison	Site 1
Site name	
Address	
Phone	
Email	
Website	
Contact person	
Available for my wedding?	
What times are available?	
Rental fee	
How many guests can the site accommodate?	
Cancellation policy	
Can I bring a caterer?	
Can I bring alcohol?	
Can I bring a wedding cake?	
Ample parking?	
Parking fees – valet parking / self-parking	
Includes seating?	
Seating rental fees	
If outdoors, is there a good indoor backup?	
How long before the reception can I set up?	
How many hours can I use the site?	
If I want to stay longer, what fees will I incur?	

Reception Site Comparison (continued)	Site 1
[1]What is the food and beverage minimum?	
[2]What is the minimum fee per person?	
[3]How is the bar fee charged?	
What is included in the package?	
• Hors d'oeuvres?	
• Open bar?	
• Courses for meal?	
• Cake?	
• Linens?	
• Centerpieces?	
• Overnight stay for bride and groom?	
What is the guest room rate?	
[4]Reserve a room without attrition clause?	
How do I rate this site? (circle one)	No way Almost Perfect Perfect!

[1] Many locations won't charge a fee to use the space, but will charge a food and beverage minimum instead. This charge is the total dollar amount you have to spend before adding service charges and taxes. These locations typically don't let you bring outside food and beverage.

[2] Some locations that have a food and beverage minimum also have a minimum per person charge. For example, if wedding menus start at $100 per person, and there is a $15,000 food and beverage minimum, you could host 150 guests at $100 each to meet the minimum requirement. You could <u>not</u> host 300 guests at $50 each.

[3] Bar fees can be tabulated a few different ways. The first is a hosted hourly bar. You will pay a fee, per person, per hour, no matter how much alcohol your guests drink. You will know exactly how much your bar will cost. The other way bar fees are tabulated is based on consumption. This means you pay for exactly what your guests drink. You will not know what your bar bill will be until the end of the night. This could be a very unpleasant surprise!

[4] An attrition clause in your contract states that if your guests don't take a certain percentage of rooms in your block, you are responsible for paying for them. For example, if you reserve 20 rooms for your wedding night, but only 13 rooms are taken, you will have to pay for the remaining 7 rooms. Most hotels allow you to reserve up to 10 rooms without an attrition clause.

Reception Site Comparison	Site 2
Site name	
Address	
Phone	
Email	
Website	
Contact person	
Available for my wedding?	
What times are available?	
Rental fee	
How many guests can the site accommodate?	
Cancellation policy	
Can I bring a caterer?	
Can I bring alcohol?	
Can I bring a wedding cake?	
Ample parking?	
Parking fees – valet parking / self-parking	
Includes seating?	
Seating rental fees	
If outdoors, is there a good indoor backup?	
How long before the reception can I set up?	
How many hours can I use the site?	
If I want to stay longer, what fees will I incur?	

Reception Site Comparison (continued)	Site 2
[1]What is the food and beverage minimum?	
[2]What is the minimum fee per person?	
[3]How is the bar fee charged?	
What is included in the package?	
• Hors d'oeuvres?	
• Open bar?	
• Courses for meal?	
• Cake?	
• Linens?	
• Centerpieces?	
• Overnight stay for bride and groom?	
What is the guest room rate?	
[4]Reserve a room without attrition clause?	
How do I rate this site? (circle one)	No way Almost Perfect Perfect!

[1] Many locations won't charge a fee to use the space, but will charge a food and beverage minimum instead. This charge is the total dollar amount you have to spend before adding service charges and taxes. These locations typically don't let you bring outside food and beverage.

[2] Some locations that have a food and beverage minimum also have a minimum per person charge. For example, if wedding menus start at $100 per person, and there is a $15,000 food and beverage minimum, you could host 150 guests at $100 each to meet the minimum requirement. You could not host 300 guests at $50 each.

[3] Bar fees can be tabulated a few different ways. The first is a hosted hourly bar. You will pay a fee, per person, per hour, no matter how much alcohol your guests drink. You will know exactly how much your bar will cost. The other way bar fees are tabulated is based on consumption. This means you pay for exactly what your guests drink. You will not know what your bar bill will be until the end of the night. This could be a very unpleasant surprise!

[4] An attrition clause in your contract states that if your guests don't take a certain percentage of rooms in your block, you are responsible for paying for them. For example, if you reserve 20 rooms for your wedding night, but only 13 rooms are taken, you will have to pay for the remaining 7 rooms. Most hotels allow you to reserve up to 10 rooms without an attrition clause.

Reception Site Comparison	Site 3
Site name	
Address	
Phone	
Email	
Website	
Contact person	
Available for my wedding?	
What times are available?	
Rental fee	
How many guests can the site accommodate?	
Cancellation policy	
Can I bring a caterer?	
Can I bring alcohol?	
Can I bring a wedding cake?	
Ample parking?	
Parking fees – valet parking / self-parking	
Includes seating?	
Seating rental fees	
If outdoors, is there a good indoor backup?	
How long before the reception can I set up?	
How many hours can I use the site?	
If I want to stay longer, what fees will I incur?	

Reception Site Comparison (continued)	Site 3
[1]What is the food and beverage minimum?	
[2]What is the minimum fee per person?	
[3]How is the bar fee charged?	
What is included in the package?	
• Hors d'oeuvres?	
• Open bar?	
• Courses for meal?	
• Cake?	
• Linens?	
• Centerpieces?	
• Overnight stay for bride and groom?	
What is the guest room rate?	
[4]Reserve a room without attrition clause?	
How do I rate this site? (circle one)	No way Almost Perfect Perfect!

[1] Many locations won't charge a fee to use the space, but will charge a food and beverage minimum instead. This charge is the total dollar amount you have to spend before adding service charges and taxes. These locations typically don't let you bring outside food and beverage.

[2] Some locations that have a food and beverage minimum also have a minimum per person charge. For example, if wedding menus start at $100 per person, and there is a $15,000 food and beverage minimum, you could host 150 guests at $100 each to meet the minimum requirement. You could not host 300 guests at $50 each.

[3] Bar fees can be tabulated a few different ways. The first is a hosted hourly bar. You will pay a fee, per person, per hour, no matter how much alcohol your guests drink. You will know exactly how much your bar will cost. The other way bar fees are tabulated is based on consumption. This means you pay for exactly what your guests drink. You will not know what your bar bill will be until the end of the night. This could be a very unpleasant surprise!

[4] An attrition clause in your contract states that if your guests don't take a certain percentage of rooms in your block, you are responsible for paying for them. For example, if you reserve 20 rooms for your wedding night, but only 13 rooms are taken, you will have to pay for the remaining 7 rooms. Most hotels allow you to reserve up to 10 rooms without an attrition clause.

Choosing Your Photographer and Videographer

These are fun and relatively easy categories to hire. First, check your budget. You don't want to fall in love with a photographer or videographer you can't afford. Take the time to look at many albums, especially albums of full weddings rather than just samples of different weddings. Also, if you are considering a company that has several photographers, make sure you view albums by the photographer that will be shooting your wedding. Include the name of your photographer in your final contract.

Photographer Comparison	Photographer 1
Name of photographer	
Address	
Phone	
Email	
Website	
Contact person	
Available for my wedding?	
Type (traditional or photojournalistic?)	
Why do you like photographing weddings?	
What's most challenging about it?	
Are you familiar with my wedding site?	
Do you have photos of my wedding site?	
Do you mind working with videographers?	
Do you mind if my guests take photos?	
Will you post my photos online?	
Will you email web-ready photos to me?	
Price range	
Hours included	
Album size included	

Photographer Comparison (continued)	Photographer 1
Do you provide high-resolution DVD?	
Overtime charges	
Bridal portrait sitting	
Engagement photos	
Number of photographers	
Payment schedule	
Method of payment	
Time for album delivery	
[1]Will you accept a photo list?	
How do I rate this photographer? (circle one)	No way Almost Perfect Perfect!

[1] When it comes to a photo list, I suggest treading lightly. Professional photographers know which photos are critical, like bride and groom with wedding party, bride and groom with parents, etc. However, I do suggest providing the photographer with the *Important Photo List* located in the back of this book.

Photographer Comparison	Photographer 2
Name of photographer	
Address	
Phone	
Email	
Website	
Contact person	
Available for my wedding?	
Type (traditional or photojournalistic?)	
Why do you like photographing weddings?	
What's most challenging about it?	
Are you familiar with my wedding site?	
Do you have photos of my wedding site?	
Do you mind working with videographers?	
Do you mind if my guests take photos?	
Will you post my photos online?	
Will you email web-ready photos to me?	
Price range	
Hours included	
Album size included	

Photographer Comparison (continued)	**Photographer 2**		
Do you provide high-resolution DVD?			
Overtime charges			
Bridal portrait sitting			
Engagement photos			
Number of photographers			
Payment schedule			
Method of payment			
Time for album delivery			
[1]Will you accept a photo list?			
How do I rate this photographer? (circle one)	No way	Almost Perfect	Perfect!

[1] When it comes to a photo list, I suggest treading lightly. Professional photographers know which photos are critical, like bride and groom with wedding party, bride and groom with parents, etc. However, I do suggest providing the photographer with the *Important Photo List* located in the back of this book.

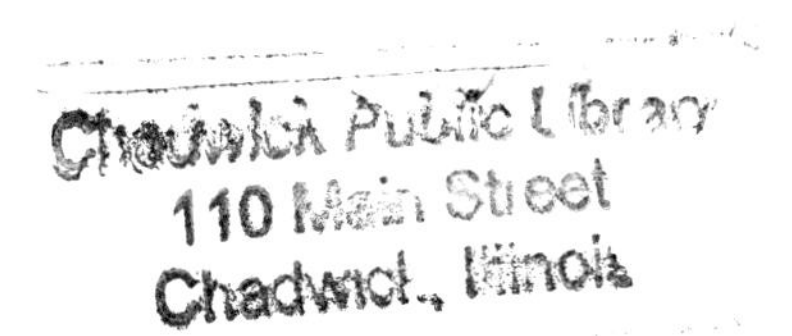

Photographer Comparison	Photographer 3
Name of photographer	
Address	
Phone	
Email	
Website	
Contact person	
Available for my wedding?	
Type (traditional or photojournalistic?)	
Why do you like photographing weddings?	
What's most challenging about it?	
Are you familiar with my wedding site?	
Do you have photos of my wedding site?	
Do you mind working with videographers?	
Do you mind if my guests take photos?	
Will you post my photos online?	
Will you email web-ready photos to me?	
Price range	
Hours included	
Album size included	

Photographer Comparison (continued)	Photographer 3
Do you provide high-resolution DVD?	
Overtime charges	
Bridal portrait sitting	
Engagement photos	
Number of photographers	
Payment schedule	
Method of payment	
Time for album delivery	
[1]Will you accept a photo list?	
How do I rate this photographer? (circle one)	No way Almost Perfect Perfect!

[1] When it comes to a photo list, I suggest treading lightly. Professional photographers know which photos are critical, like bride and groom with wedding party, bride and groom with parents, etc. However, I do suggest providing the photographer with the *Important Photo List* located in the back of this book.

Videographer Comparison	Videographer 1
Name of videographer	
Address	
Phone	
Email	
Website	
Contact person	
Available for my wedding?	
Type of videographer	
Why do you like filming weddings?	
What's most challenging about it?	
Are you familiar with my wedding site?	
Do you have videos of my wedding site?	
Do you mind if my guests take video?	
Price range	
Hours included	
[1]Editing features	
Number of shooters	
Number of DVDs	
Will you post a video clip online?	
Will you email a web-ready video clip to me?	

Videographer Comparison (continued)	Videographer 1
Photo montage included?	
May I select music for DVD?	
Guest interviews at the wedding?	
Overtime charges	
Payment schedule	
Method of payment	
Time for DVD delivery	
Will you accept a video list?	
How do I rate this videographer? (circle one)	No way Almost Perfect Perfect!

[1] Some videographers do very little editing and hand over a video with hours of footage; others edit down the day to a single hour. Some use a lot of special effects, and others keep it clean. Make sure you view a full wedding video so you can determine which style you like.

Videographer Comparison	Videographer 2
Name of videographer	
Address	
Phone	
Email	
Website	
Contact person	
Available for my wedding?	
Type of videographer	
Why do you like filming weddings?	
What's most challenging about it?	
Are you familiar with my wedding site?	
Do you have videos of my wedding site?	
Do you mind if my guests take video?	
Price range	
Hours included	
[1]Editing features	
Number of shooters	
Number of DVDs	
Will you post a video clip online?	
Will you email a web-ready video clip to me?	

Videographer Comparison (continued)	Videographer 2
Photo montage included?	
May I select music for DVD?	
Guest interviews at the wedding?	
Overtime charges	
Payment schedule	
Method of payment	
Time for DVD delivery	
Will you accept a video list?	
How do I rate this videographer? (circle one)	No way Almost Perfect Perfect!

[1] Some videographers do very little editing and hand over a video with hours of footage; others edit down the day to a single hour. Some use a lot of special effects, and others keep it clean. Make sure you view a full wedding video so you can determine which style you like.

Videographer Comparison	Videographer 3
Name of videographer	
Address	
Phone	
Email	
Website	
Contact person	
Available for my wedding?	
Type of videographer	
Why do you like filming weddings?	
What's most challenging about it?	
Are you familiar with my wedding site?	
Do you have videos of my wedding site?	
Do you mind if my guests take video?	
Price range	
Hours included	
[1]Editing features	
Number of shooters	
Number of DVDs	
Will you post a video clip online?	
Will you email a web-ready video clip to me?	

Videographer Comparison (continued)	Videographer 3
Photo montage included?	
May I select music for DVD?	
Guest interviews at the wedding?	
Overtime charges	
Payment schedule	
Method of payment	
Time for DVD delivery	
Will you accept a video list?	
How do I rate this videographer? (circle one)	No way Almost Perfect Perfect!

[1] Some videographers do very little editing and hand over a video with hours of footage; others edit down the day to a single hour. Some use a lot of special effects, and others keep it clean. Make sure you view a full wedding video so you can determine which style you like.

Choosing Your Florist

Florists have many different styles and price ranges. Make sure you look at each florist's portfolio to see if her design style matches your vision for your wedding day. Also, be very upfront about your floral budget and see if the florist is able to help you achieve the look you want for the price you can afford. Most importantly, make sure the florist listens to you. You don't want to hire a florist who isn't paying attention to what you want on your wedding day!

Florist Comparison	Florist 1
Name of florist	
Address	
Phone	
Email	
Website	
Contact person	
Available for my wedding?	
Favorite style of wedding?	
Are you familiar with my wedding site?	
Do you have photos at my wedding site?	
Will you prepare a sample centerpiece?	
Separate fees for delivery and set up?	
Do you help with linen/lighting/foliage rental?	
Can you work within my budget?	
Do you have ideas to save money on décor?	
Payment schedule	
Method of payment	
How long do you need for set up?	
How do I rate this florist? (circle one)	No way Almost Perfect Perfect!

Florist Comparison	Florist 2
Name of florist	
Address	
Phone	
Email	
Website	
Contact person	
Available for my wedding?	
Favorite style of wedding?	
Are you familiar with my wedding site?	
Do you have photos at my wedding site?	
Will you prepare a sample centerpiece?	
Separate fees for delivery and set up?	
Do you help with linen/lighting/foliage rental?	
Can you work within my budget?	
Do you have ideas to save money on décor?	
Payment schedule	
Method of payment	
How long do you need for set up?	
How do I rate this florist? (circle one)	No way Almost Perfect Perfect!

Florist Comparison	Florist 3
Name of florist	
Address	
Phone	
Email	
Website	
Contact person	
Available for my wedding?	
Favorite style of wedding?	
Are you familiar with my wedding site?	
Do you have photos at my wedding site?	
Will you prepare a sample centerpiece?	
Separate fees for delivery and set up?	
Do you help with linen/lighting/foliage rental?	
Can you work within my budget?	
Do you have ideas to save money on décor?	
Payment schedule	
Method of payment	
How long do you need for set up?	
How do I rate this florist? (circle one)	No way Almost Perfect Perfect!

Choosing Musicians

You will need to have music for your ceremony, cocktail hour, and reception. You may achieve this through live musicians, a DJ, and sometimes, for cocktail hour, you can use piped-in music provided by your reception venue. When choosing live musicians, look for talent and personality. For ceremony music, the most cost effective method is to hire your DJ for an extra hour to play for the ceremony. If you want live music for your ceremony, some of my favorites include harpists, string quartets, and flute quartets. For a dramatic touch, consider adding bagpipes, a trumpet, or a choir.

Ceremony Musician Comparison	Musician 1
Name of musician	
Address	
Phone	
Email	
Website	
Contact person	
Available for my wedding?	
Will you help select my music?	
If I want a certain song, will you learn it?	
Is there a fee for learning/buying new music?	
What are your electrical requirements?	
Are you willing to play outdoors?	
Restrictions for outdoor ceremonies	
Do you have a demo?	
Can you work within my budget?	
Payment schedule	
Method of payment	
How long do you need for set up?	
How do I rate this musician? (circle one)	No way Almost Perfect Perfect!

Ceremony Musician Comparison	Musician 2
Name of musician	
Address	
Phone	
Email	
Website	
Contact person	
Available for my wedding?	
Will you help select my music?	
If I want a certain song, will you learn it?	
Is there a fee for learning/buying new music?	
What are your electrical requirements?	
Are you willing to play outdoors?	
Restrictions for outdoor ceremonies	
Do you have a demo?	
Can you work within my budget?	
Payment schedule	
Method of payment	
How long do you need for set up?	
How do I rate this musician? (circle one)	No way Almost Perfect Perfect!

Ceremony Musician Comparison	Musician 3
Name of musician	
Address	
Phone	
Email	
Website	
Contact person	
Available for my wedding?	
Will you help select my music?	
If I want a certain song, will you learn it?	
Is there a fee for learning/buying new music?	
What are your electrical requirements?	
Are you willing to play outdoors?	
Restrictions for outdoor ceremonies	
Do you have a demo?	
Can you work within my budget?	
Payment schedule	
Method of payment	
How long do you need for set up?	
How do I rate this musician? (circle one)	No way Almost Perfect Perfect!

Whether your reception music is live or you hire a DJ, your reception entertainment will make the difference between a reception that's a "Wow," or a reception that's humdrum. Both options are good, but when it comes to budget, DJs are more cost effective than a full band. Whichever you decide to use, make sure to meet the DJ or band leader in person to make sure he or she matches your vision and style.

Reception Musician Comparison	Musician 1
Name of musician/DJ	
Address	
Phone	
Email	
Website	
Contact person	
Available for my wedding?	
Will you help select my music?	
Will you help plan reception activities?	
Performance style (low key or lots of talking?)	
How do you get guests interested in dancing?	
If I want a certain song, will you learn it?	
Is there a fee for learning/buying new music?	
What are your electrical requirements?	
Are you willing to play outdoors?	
Restrictions for outdoor ceremonies	
Do you have a demo?	
Can you work within my budget?	
Payment schedule	
Method of payment	
How long do you need for set up?	
How do I rate this musician? (circle one)	No way Almost Perfect Perfect!

Reception Musician Comparison	Musician 2
Name of musician/DJ	
Address	
Phone	
Email	
Website	
Contact person	
Available for my wedding?	
Will you help select my music?	
Will you help plan reception activities?	
Performance style (low key or lots of talking?)	
How do you get guests interested in dancing?	
If I want a certain song, will you learn it?	
Is there a fee for learning/buying new music?	
What are your electrical requirements?	
Are you willing to play outdoors?	
Restrictions for outdoor ceremonies	
Do you have a demo?	
Can you work within my budget?	
Payment schedule	
Method of payment	
How long do you need for set up?	
How do I rate this musician? (circle one)	No way Almost Perfect Perfect!

Reception Musician Comparison	Musician 3
Name of musician/DJ	
Address	
Phone	
Email	
Website	
Contact person	
Available for my wedding?	
Will you help select my music?	
Will you help plan reception activities?	
Performance style (low key or lots of talking?)	
How do you get guests interested in dancing?	
If I want a certain song, will you learn it?	
Is there a fee for learning/buying new music?	
What are your electrical requirements?	
Are you willing to play outdoors?	
Restrictions for outdoor ceremonies	
Do you have a demo?	
Can you work within my budget?	
Payment schedule	
Method of payment	
How long do you need for set up?	
How do I rate this musician? (circle one)	No way Almost Perfect Perfect!

Purchasing Your Wedding Attire

This section is more about advice than a checklist. Of course, you will need to know the price of your gown and the fees for alteration, but purchasing a wedding gown and bridesmaids' dresses is more about finding the look you love.

- Before going shopping, look on the internet and in magazines to find photos of styles you like. Tear out or print these photos. Keep in mind, the women wearing the gowns in the magazines are very tall and thin. The styles that you like in print may not be right for your stature and figure, so go to the salon with an open mind and try on several styles.

- I suggest not taking a crowd with you when you begin trying on wedding gowns and bridesmaids' dresses. Having too many opinions can get confusing. You want to make sure you get the gown and dresses *you* love, not that your friends love (although finding one that fits both categories is always nice). So grab your mom, your best friend, or your bridesmaid with the quirkiest figure, and head out to your favorite salon!

- When you go shopping, dress the part. Wear good foundation garments and shoes with the heel-height that you will most likely wear on your wedding day.

- Tell the gown consultant your budget. Ask her to not show you gowns and dresses that would cause you to overspend.

- Listen to suggestions from the salon gown consultant. Over the years, I have found they have a knack for choosing just the right style.

- Make sure the gown consultant takes your measurements. She should show you the sizing chart from the gown manufacturer and explain how she decided which size to order for you (typically the size is based on your largest measurement).

- You will also need the following information: What types of payment does the salon accept? How long will it take the gown to arrive? Does the salon have on-site alterations? How much are the alteration fees? How long will alterations take?

- Once you narrow down your gown and dress choices, feel free to bring other friends to help you choose "the one."

Finding the Special Touches

There are so many wonderful options for adding your special signature to your wedding. There are countless websites with wedding favor and décor ideas. I suggest reading other brides' blogs for ideas, too. It's fun to see what other couples did on their wedding day (and to get insight on what worked and what didn't). Below is some additional insight on adding special touches to your wedding:

- What are some things that you and your fiancé are known for? You can get inspiration from your ethnic backgrounds, favorite restaurants, hobbies, and careers.

- Consider making a charitable contribution or giving something back to your community in lieu of favors. Write a story about why you chose the particular charity or cause, and display it for your guests to see. Who knows, you might inspire one of your guests to take up that cause as well! Can you think of a more personal or meaningful way to start your life together?

- If you are going to be designing and putting together your favors, make sure to give yourself enough time. You don't want to go crazy the week of your wedding!

Negotiating Contracts

As you find locations and vendors you like, you will need to negotiate and sign contracts. Do not hire any vendor based on a verbal agreement. Everything must be written in a contract. Here are my suggestions for items to look for in your contracts:

- Correct date, day of week, time, and location of your wedding

- Name of the vendor who will be working at your wedding

- Contact information for the vendor on your wedding day. This means a cell phone number!

- All fees, including optional overtime

- Methods of payment accepted

- Dates of when payment installments are due
- Exact services you are contracting. If the vendor's contract doesn't include this information, ask to attach the vendor's brochure or information sheet to the contract.
- When final products will be delivered
- Once you sign the contract, make sure the vendor signs it, too, and provides you with a copy of the contract showing both signatures.

Now it's time to get organized!

Part 3: Organizing

The big day is approaching! At this point, you must be incredibly anxious about all the tasks and items that need to be organized before your wedding day. This section will help you get all your months of planning – the notes, ideas, and contracts – organized so that someone other than you can execute your wedding day. Let's begin by creating your final payment list.

Take out all of your contracts and lay them on the table in front of you. Each contract has different payment requirements. You are going to chart your contracts so that you can pay them properly and on time. Fill out the information below, then get ready to write checks or submit online payments.

Vendor Contracts

Vendor Name ______________________ Total fee ________

Method of payment ________ Deposit ________ Balance ________ Balance paid ________

Vendor Name ______________________ Total fee ________

Method of payment ________ Deposit ________ Balance ________ Balance paid ________

Vendor Name ______________________ Total fee ________

Method of payment ________ Deposit ________ Balance ________ Balance paid ________

Vendor Name ______________________ Total fee ________

Method of payment ________ Deposit ________ Balance ________ Balance paid ________

Vendor Name ______________________ Total fee ________

Method of payment ________ Deposit ________ Balance ________ Balance paid ________

Vendor Contracts

Vendor Name ________________________ Total fee __________

Method of payment ________ Deposit ________ Balance ________ Balance paid ________

Vendor Name ________________________ Total fee __________

Method of payment ________ Deposit ________ Balance ________ Balance paid ________

Vendor Name ________________________ Total fee __________

Method of payment ________ Deposit ________ Balance ________ Balance paid ________

Vendor Name ________________________ Total fee __________

Method of payment ________ Deposit ________ Balance ________ Balance paid ________

Vendor Name ________________________ Total fee __________

Method of payment ________ Deposit ________ Balance ________ Balance paid ________

Vendor Name ________________________ Total fee __________

Method of payment ________ Deposit ________ Balance ________ Balance paid ________

Vendor Name ________________________ Total fee __________

Method of payment ________ Deposit ________ Balance ________ Balance paid ________

Wedding Week Agenda

The following wedding week agenda will serve as a reminder of when final counts are due, when set up is available, and even when you would like to toss your bouquet and garter. The agenda included on the next few pages is an example you can use. You may have other ideas as to the items you want included on your wedding day. There is no right or wrong answer, just make sure whatever you want to have happen on your wedding day, happens!

Wedding Week Agenda	
Time	**Action Item**
	Three Weeks Prior – Week of ___________
___________	Final guest count to the cake designer
___________	Marriage license has been obtained
	Two Weeks Prior – Week of ___________
___________	Final count to the florist for centerpieces
___________	All attendants' gifts are purchased and wrapped
___________	Send first version of agenda to vendors
	One Week Prior – Week of ___________
___________	Final guest count to caterer
___________	Confirm all wedding vendors
	Rehearsal Day
___________	All transportation is confirmed
___________	Tuxedo pickup
___________	All wedding participants arrive for rehearsal
___________	All wedding-related items given to person in charge
___________	Marriage license given to officiant
___________	Rehearsal begins
___________	Rehearsal concludes
___________	Rehearsal dinner begins

Wedding Week Agenda (continued)

Time	Action Item
	Wedding Day
____________	Room set up begins
____________	Florist arrives for set up
____________	Linens arrive for steam
____________	Hairstyling begins
____________	Videographer arrives for set up
____________	Photographer arrives for set up
____________	Musician/DJ arrives for set up
____________	Groom and groomsmen arrive at ceremony site
____________	Videographer and photographer begin pre-wedding footage
____________	All ceremony set up is complete
____________	Groomsmen, ushers, and program attendants take their places
____________	Sound check for DJ and officiant is complete
____________	Prelude music begins
____________	Parents greet guests at entrance to ceremony
____________	Guest arrival begins
____________	Pre-wedding photos conclude
____________	Bride and wedding party to be prepared for processional
____________	Ceremony begins
____________	Cocktail hour set up is complete
____________	Reception set up is complete
____________	Catering staff is ready for guest arrival at cocktail hour
____________	Ceremony concludes
____________	Post-wedding photos begin
____________	Guests make their way to cocktail hour
____________	Floral arrangements to be moved to reception site by florist

Wedding Week Agenda (continued)

Time	Action Item
	***Wedding Day** (continued)*
________	Post-wedding photos conclude
________	DJ and catering staff ready for guests to move to reception area
________	Cocktail reception ends
________	DJ begins playing
________	Staff invites guests to move to reception area
________	Champagne is poured for toasts
________	Wedding party, bride, and groom are introduced into reception
________	Bride and groom's first dance (name of song)
	________________________
________	Bride's father gives welcome greeting to guests
________	Best man gives toast, then maid of honor gives toast
________	Blessing is given by officant
________	Dinner is served
________	DJ announces buffet stations are open and what is at each station
________	Dinner concludes
________	Father/daughter dance (name of song)
	________________________
________	Mother/son dance (name of song)
	________________________
________	Cake cutting (name of song)
	________________________
________	Dance, Dance, Dance!
________	Garter and bouquet toss (name of song)
	________________________
________	Departure transportation arrives
________	Last dance/reception concludes

Wedding Week Agenda (continued)

Time | **Action Item**

Wedding Day *(continued)*

____________ Bride and groom depart

____________ Post-reception breakdown/gifts delivered to ____________________

____________ Food and cake packed and delivered to ______________________

After the Wedding Day

____________ Brunch

____________ Honeymoon transportation departs

Wedding Related Items (initials of person responsible)

Ceremony

Programs ______

Gift card box ______

Cocktail hour

Escort cards ______

Escort card board ______

Bathrooms ______

Amenity baskets ______

Reception

Cake knife & server ______

Champagne flutes ______

Sparklers ______

Table numbers ______

Candy station items ______

Cupcake pails ______

Additional Action Items

____

____

____

____

____

____

Important Photo List

Most wedding photographers don't like getting shot lists. They know to take a photo of the bride and groom, the bride and groom with her parents, the groom with his parents, etc. However, I think it is important to provide the photographer with a list of photos that he or she might not anticipate. For example, if your best friend from kindergarten is going to attend your wedding and you want a photo with her, the photographer needs to know. If you and your siblings have taken the same type of photograph at every family gathering, the photographer needs to know about it. I suggest putting together a shot list of those unusual photographs and handing it to the photographer at your last planning meeting, or have the person in charge do it for you on your wedding day. Try not to make it too long or complicated. You don't want to spend your wedding day taking photos for hours at a time!

Seating List

Once all your invitation responses come back, you will need to make a few different seating lists for your catering manager. One list will be an alphabetical list (by last name) of your guests and their table numbers. This will allow the catering staff to assist your guests when they need to find their tables. You should also add any special requests to the list (see examples on following page). Also, if your guests chose what entrée they will be eating, you are going to need a list of your guests by table, along with their entree selections. An example of each list is provided.

Alphabetical Guest List – Table Numbers

Guest	Table Number	Special Requests
A		
Mr. and Mrs. John Adams	2	
Mr. and Mrs. Scott Alexander	4	Vegetarian
B		
Mr. and Mrs. Steven Brown	4	
C		
Mr. and Mrs. David Cohen	3	Guest in wheelchair
Mr. and Mrs. Sam Covel	5	High chair

Alphabetical Guest List – Food Selections

Table 1	
Mr. and Mrs. John Adams	Chicken and Beef
Mr. and Mrs. Scott Davis	Chicken and Chicken
Mr. and Mrs. David Frankel	Beef and Beef
Dr. and Mrs. Alexander Smith	Chicken and Vegetarian

When your guests make entrée selections in advance of your wedding day, you will likely need to provide a card for each guest indicating whether the guest is eating beef, chicken, fish, or vegetarian. Some of my brides have used decorative symbols, like a star for beef, a square for chicken, a circle for fish, and a triangle for vegetarian. Others prefer to use B, C, F, or V on the card. Be sure to check with your catering manager for guidelines.

Announcement List

This is where your wedding party contact list comes in handy. Take the list from the pre-planning section and pair your bridesmaids and groomsmen as you want to see them walking up the aisle. Now put them together in a list like the one below.

Make sure your list has the names written exactly as each member of your wedding party wants to be introduced. Also, if any members of your wedding party have a difficult name to pronounce, spell it phonetically on the list.

Announcement List
Mother and Father of the Bride
Mother and Father of the Groom
Flower Girl and Ring Bearer
Bridesmaids and Groomsmen
Maid of Honor and Best Man
Bride and Groom

Inventory List

If you want to be able to relax and enjoy your wedding day, it is very important that you take an inventory of all the items you want to set out for your ceremony and reception. Favors, toasting glasses, cake knife and server, photos, sign-in books, etc., must all be on this list. Furthermore, if you have a specific manner in which you would like these items displayed, you should write that directly on the list provided so that whomever is in charge will know exactly where you would like them without having to disturb you.

Inventory List

Ceremony

________	Unity candle	________	Flower arrangements
________	Sand ceremony items	________	Ring bearer pillow
________	Guest book and pen	________	Flower girl basket
________	Pew bows	________	Leftover programs

Reception

________	Engagement/bridal portrait	________	Flower arrangements
________	Leftover personalized napkins	________	Your bouquet
________	Leftover favors	________	Money bag, box, bird cage, etc.
________	Leftover tossing items	________	Wedding gown
________	Disposable cameras	________	Groom's tuxedo
________	Toasting flutes	________	CDs/DVDs you provided
________	Cake knife and server	________	Wedding gifts
________	Cake top ornament	________	Family photos
________	Top layer of cake	________	Ketubah
________	Cake parts other than top	________	Kiddish cup
________	Leftover cake/groom's cake	________	Glass shards from glass-breaking
________	Centerpieces	________	Other

I have inventoried all items checked above and accounted for them ____________________
(signature of coordinator on duty)

I was not able to account for the following items ______________________________

____

Well, there you have it – three big steps to planning your perfect wedding. Of course, there are many details you will fill in as you meet vendors and get new ideas. Each vendor you meet will inspire something you hadn't thought of before. Just keep taking notes and go down your checklist. If you work a little each day, the task of planning your wedding won't be as daunting as you might have initially thought.

My last bit of advice for you is to plan your wedding, hand it over to someone you trust, then relax and enjoy! You won't believe how quickly your special day will fly. Don't let any little mishaps or misunderstandings bother you. If your bouquet is light pink instead of medium fuchsia, let it go. If your maid of honor wears her hair down instead of up, forget about it. Nothing should stand in the way of you reveling in each special moment of your wedding day.

Remember, *Perfect Wedding Guide* and I are always available resources. Keep going back to *PerfectWeddingGuide.com* for the latest in wedding industry trends, and go to my blog at *PerfectWeddingGuide.com/Wedding-Blog/* and feel free to send me an email at susan.southerland@pwg.com.

Happy Planning!

My Wedding Profile

89

Wedding Profile

Bride and Groom		**Wedding Date**	
________		________	
Vendors			
Ceremony site	________	Entertainment	________
Reception site	________	Floral	________
Photography	________	Bakery	________
Videography	________	Wedding planner	________
Guests			
No. of guests	________	Room list	________
Room block	________	Room amenities	________
Rehearsal			
Time	________	Officiant attending	________
Items needed	________	Other	________
Rehearsal Dinner			
Location	________	Décor	________
Time	________	Transportation	________
Confirmed Res?	________	Other	________
Formalwear			
Bridal gown	________	Steaming	________
Bridesmaids	________	Dressing where?	________
Tuxedos	________	Other	________
Personal Floral			
Bride	________	Corsages	________
Groom	________	Flower girl	________
Bouquets	________	Other	________
Photography			
Special request	________	Location	________

Wedding Profile (continued)

Videography

Special request	______	Other	______

Ceremony

Location	______	Marriage license	______
Time	______	Programs	______
Guest parking	______	Transportation	______
Special seating	______	Other	______

Cocktail Reception

Cocktail hour	______	Gift card box	______
Guest parking	______	Guest book table	______
Entertainment	______	Other	______
Gift table	______	Other	______

Reception Set

Color of linen	______	Place cards	______
Rental linen	______	Place card table	______
Napkin fold	______	Guest book table	______
Centerpieces	______	Gift table	______
Dance floor	______	Cake table	______
Rental staging	______	Cake design	______
Cake boxes	______	Cake topper	______
No. of tables	______	Bride/groom seat	______
Tables Nos.	______	Groom cake design	______
Guests/table	______	Groom cake table	______
Favors	______	Cake knife/server	______
Flutes	______	Other	______
Tenting/heater	______	Other	______

Wedding Profile (continued)

Reception

Reception time	______	No. vendor meals	______
Dinner time	______	Special diet needs	______
Dances	______	Cake cutting time	______
Special events	______	Last dance time	______
Toast time	______	Grand exit	______
No. adult meals	______	Transportation	______
No. child meals	______	Other	______

Post-Wedding

Clean up	______	Events for guests	______
Suite reserved	______	Day-after bunch	______

Wedding Planner Tasks

______

______

______

______

______

______

______

Special Notes

______

______

______

______

______

______

______

About the Author

As one of the foremost experts in the wedding industry, Susan Southerland is one of the nation's top wedding planners. Her experience includes planning thousands of weddings around the world, in which she and her team carefully execute each detail with passion and precision. Susan is owner and president of *Just Marry!*, with home offices in Central Florida. She focuses on all weddings, from intimate to extravagant, from cultural to destination, making memories of a lifetime.

Susan's exceptional weddings have been featured numerous times on Style Network's *Whose Wedding Is It Anyway?* and TLC's *A Wedding Story*, Her cutting edge advice has been featured in television broadcasts and periodicals around the world, including *Destination Weddings and Honeymoons Magazine*, *The Wall Street Journal*, *The New York Times,* and *USA Today*.

Admired for her depth of knowledge and her easygoing personality, Susan boasts the honor of being the official National Wedding Expert for *Perfect Wedding Guide*. In addition to the *Susan Southerland Secret* website, Susan's advice can be found on *PerfectWeddingGuide.com*.

Here's where you can find Susan Southerland wedding planning products and wedding advice!

Websites & Blog

- *Just Marry!* – JustMarry.com
- *The Susan Southerland Secret* – SusanSoutherland.com
- *Perfect Wedding Guide Wedding Blog* – PerfectWeddingGuide.com/Wedding-Blog

Wedding Planning Products

- *Susan Southerland's Just Marry! Wedding Planning Secrets DVD*
  http://tinyurl.com/4sjst4x
- *Susan Southerland's Just Marry! Wedding Color Selection Wheel*
  http://tinyurl.com/29fuvfe

Twitter
Twitter.com/SusanSoutherlan
Twitter.com/PerfectWedding
Twitter.com/JustMarryInc

Facebook
Facbook.com/SusanSoutherlandSecret
Facebook.com/JustMarry
Facebook.com/PerfectWeddingGuide

My Notes

Index

A

Accessories, 34
Agenda, 3, 80-83
Aisle runner, 14, 18
Alcohol, 46-51
Altar arrangement, 14, 18
Alterations, 14, 18, 73
Announcement list, 3, 86
Announcements, 16, 20, 33
Attendants, 15, 18, 28, 80-81
Attire restrictions, 41, 43, 45
Attrition clause, 47, 49, 51
Audio equipment, 41, 43, 45

B

Ballroom, 26
Band, 33, 70
Bar, 16, 19, 47, 49, 51
Bar fee, 47, 49, 51
Beach, 6, 26-27
Best man, 15, 19, 29, 82, 86
Bird cage, 87
Blog, 3, 74, 88, 93
Bouquet, 15, 18-19, 80, 82, 87-88, 90
Boutonniere, 15, 19
Bridal attire, 14, 18
Bridal party accessories, 34
Bridal portrait, 15, 19, 53, 55, 57, 87
Bridal registry, 34
Bridesmaid, 6, 15, 18-19, 27-32, 73, 86, 90
Bridesmaids' bouquets, 15, 19
Bridesmaids' dresses, 27, 32, 73
Bridesmaids' luncheon, 15, 18
Brunch, 7-13, 27, 83
Bubbles, 15, 19
Budget, 2-3, 6, 14, 17-21, 28, 38, 52, 64-73
Budget counselor, 21

C

Cake cutting, 82
Cake delivery, 16
Cake designer, 80
Cake flowers, 16, 19
Cake knife, 15, 18, 34, 83, 87, 91
Cake server, 34, 83, 87, 91
Cake set up, 16, 20
Cake topper, 15, 18, 91
Calligraphy, 16, 20, 33-34
Cancellation policy, 46, 48, 50
Candelabra, 41, 43, 45
Candy station, 83
Caterer, 33, 46, 48, 50, 80
Catering manager, 25, 33, 84-85
Catering staff, 81-82, 84
Centerpiece, 16, 19, 47, 49, 51, 64-66, 80, 87, 91
Ceremony, 2, 6, 14-16, 18, 20, 26-27, 33-35, 40-45, 67-69, 81, 83, 87, 90-91
Ceremony coordinator, 40-45
Ceremony decorations, 14
Ceremony musician, 33-35, 67-69
Ceremony programs, 16, 20, 33, 81, 83, 87, 91
Ceremony site, 2, 33, 40-45, 81, 90
Chairs, 14, 16, 18-19, 85
Chair decorations, 14, 18
Champagne, 82,-83
Charitable contribution, 74
Checklist, 3, 25, 32-35, 39, 73, 88
China, 16, 19
Clergy fee, 40, 42, 44
Cocktail dress, 26
Cocktail hour, 15-16, 18-19, 27, 67, 81, 83, 91
Color scheme, 6, 27, 32
Contract, 2, 25, 39, 47, 49, 51-52, 74-75, 78-79

Contract negotiation, 2, 74
Corsage, 15, 19, 90
Counseling, 15, 18, 40, 42, 44
Crinoline, 14, 18
Crystal, 16, 19
Cupcake, 83
Custodial fee, 40, 42, 44
Custodian, 15, 18

D

Dance floor, 16, 19, 91
Dance lessons, 15, 18
Dancing, 27, 70-72
Décor, 41, 43, 45, 64-66, 74, 90
Decorations, 14, 16, 18-19, 41, 43, 45
Dessert, 16, 19, 27
Dessert reception, 27
Dinner reception, 27
DJ, 33, 67, 70-72, 81-82

E

Engagement, 2, 15, 19, 32-33, 53, 55, 57, 87
Engagement photo, 15, 19, 53, 55, 57
Entertainment, 14-15, 18, 70, 90-91
Entrée, 16, 20, 84-85
Envelope liners, 16, 20
Envelopes, 16, 20, 33
Escort card, 83
Escort card board, 83

F

Father of the bride, 86
Father of the groom, 86
Favors, 15, 17-18, 34, 74, 87, 91
Fees, 22-24, 40, 42, 44, 46-51, 64-74, 78-79
Final head count, 35
First dance, 82
Floral preservation, 15, 18, 35
Florist, 2, 33-34, 64-66, 80-81
Flower girl, 15, 19, 31, 34, 86-87, 90
Flowers, 6, 14-20, 27, 87
Foliage rental, 64-66
Food and beverage, 17, 27, 47, 49, 51
Food and beverage minimum, 47, 49, 51
Formal attire, 27
Formal wedding, 27

G

Garden ceremony, 6
Gift, 7-13, 15, 18, 35, 80, 83, 87, 91
Gift card box, 83, 91
Gift for bride, 15, 18
Gift for groom, 15, 18
Gown consultant, 73
Gown preservation, 35
Groom's cake, 87, 91
Groom's boutonniere, 15, 19
Groom's ring, 15, 18
Groomsmen, 15, 19, 28-31, 33, 81, 86
Guest book, 31, 34, 87, 91
Guest book attendant, 31
Guest book table, 91
Guest list, 2-3, 6-14, 32, 85
Guest List Manager, 3, 14
Guest room, 47, 49, 51

H

Hair and makeup, 15, 18, 28, 34
Hair and makeup artist, 34
Hairstyling, 81
Head table, 16, 19
Honeymoon, 15, 18, 34, 83, 93
Hors d'oeuvres, 47, 49, 51
Hosted hourly bar, 47, 49, 51
Hotel ballroom, 26

I

Interview process, 38-39
Inventory, 3, 87
Inventory list, 3, 87
Invitations, 14, 16, 20, 28, 33-34, 84

J

Just Marry!, 1, 3, 14, 27, 93

K

Ketubah, 15, 18, 87
Kiddish cup, 87

L

Last dance, 82
Late-night dessert reception, 27
Lighting, 16, 19, 27, 64-66
Linens, 16, 19, 27, 33-34, 47, 49, 51, 64-66, 81, 91
Luncheon, 15-16, 18, 20

M

Maid of honor, 15, 19, 29, 82, 86, 88
Makeup, 15, 18, 28, 34
Map cards, 16, 20, 33
Marriage license, 15, 19, 34-35, 80, 91
Menu, 33-34, 46-47, 49, 51
Menu tasting, 34
Mother of the bride, 86
Mother of the groom, 86
Museum, 26
Music, 2, 15, 18, 33-35, 40-45, 59, 61, 63, 67-72, 81
Musician, 2, 15, 18, 33, 35, 40, 42, 44, 67-72, 81
Musician fee, 40, 42, 44

N

Napkins, 16, 20, 33, 87, 91
Negotiating contracts, 2, 74

O

Officiant, 15, 18, 34, 41, 43, 45, 80-81, 90
Organizing, 2, 77-88
Out of town guests, 33, 35
Outdoor ceremony, 67-72
Overtime charges, 53, 55, 57, 59, 61, 63

P

Pastry chef, 33
Payment schedule, 22-24, 53, 55, 57, 59, 61, 63-72
Perfect Wedding Guide, 1-3, 6, 14, 17, 21, 32, 38, 88, 93
Pew, 14, 18, 87
Pew arrangement, 14, 18
Pew bows, 87
Photo montage, 59, 61, 63
Photographer, 2, 33, 35, 52, 57, 81, 84
Photography package, 15, 19
Photojournalistic photography, 52, 54, 56
Place of worship, 26, 40-41, 43, 45
Place cards, 16, 20, 33, 35, 91
Postage, 16, 20
Prelude music, 81
Pre-marital class, 40, 42, 44
Pre-marital counseling, 40, 42, 44
Pre-planning, 2, 5-35
Programs, 16, 20, 33, 81, 83, 87, 91

Q

Questionnaire, 14-16, 25-26

R

Reader, 15, 19
Reception, 2, 15-20, 27, 33-35, 46-51, 67, 70-72, 81-83, 87, 90-91
Reception cards, 16, 20, 33
Reception decorations, 16
Reception music, 35, 70-72
Reception site, 2, 16, 19-20, 33, 46-51, 81, 90
Registry, 34
Rehearsal dinner, 7-13, 15, 19, 34, 80, 90
Rental fee, 40, 42, 44, 46, 48, 50
Response cards, 33
Return address card, 16, 20
Return address envelope, 33
Ring, 15, 18-19, 31, 34, 86-87
Ring bearer, 15, 19, 31, 45, 86-87
Ring pillow, 15, 19, 34, 87
RSVP, 14

S

Sand ceremony, 14, 18, 87
Save-the-date, 32
Seating arrangement, 35
Seating list, 3, 84
Seating rental fee, 46, 48, 50
Self-parking, 46, 48, 50
Service charge, 47, 49, 51
Shoes, 14, 18, 35, 73
Shopping, 2, 37-75
Sign-in book, 15, 19
Sizing chart, 73
Soloist, 15, 18
Sparklers, 15, 19, 83
Special requests, 84-85, 90-91
Special touches, 2, 74
Spreadsheet, 14
Stationery, 16, 20, 33
Sugar flowers, 16, 20
Sunrise wedding, 6
Sunset wedding, 6
Synagogue, 40

T

Table number, 83-85
Tax, 15-16, 19-20, 47, 49, 51
Tents, 16, 20, 91
Thank you note, 33, 35
Tip, 16, 20
Toast, 15, 19, 34, 82, 87
Top layer of cake, 87
Transportation, 7-14, 16, 20, 34-35, 80, 82-83, 90-91
Transportation inserts, 35
Trial run, 15, 18, 34
Tuxedo, 25-26, 41, 43, 45, 80, 87, 90

U

Unity candle, 14, 18, 87
Usher, 31, 81

V

Valet parking, 46, 48, 50
Veil, 14, 18
Vendor, 2-3, 6, 17, 21, 25, 35, 38-39, 41, 43, 45, 74-75, 78-80, 88, 90, 92
Video editing, 58-63
Video package, 16, 20
Videographer, 2, 33, 52, 54, 56, 58-63, 81

W - Z

Wardrobe, 27
Wedding components, 14-16
Wedding date, 2, 6, 32, 74, 90
Wedding day schedule, 35
Wedding day transportation, 34
Wedding night accommodations, 47, 49, 51
Wedding party, 2, 6, 15-16, 18, 20, 28-32, 35, 41, 43, 45, 53, 55, 57, 81-82, 86
Wedding planner, 2, 16, 20-25, 32, 34-35, 90, 92
Wedding profile, 38, 89-91
Wedding week agenda, 3, 80-83